Ripley's Believe It or Not!®

Developed and produced by Ripley Publishing Ltd

This edition published and distributed by:

 Mason Crest
450 Parkway Drive, Suite D, Broomall, PA 19008
www.masoncrest.com

Printed and bound in the United States of America

First printing
9 8 7 6 5 4 3 2 1

Ripley's Believe It or Not!
Strange Stories
ISBN: 978-1-4222-2782-4 (hardback)
ISBN: 978-1-4222-9043-9 (e-book)
Ripley's Believe It or Not!—Complete 8 Title Series
ISBN: 978-1-4222-2979-8

Cataloging-in-Publication Data on file with the Library of Congress

PUBLISHER'S NOTE
While every effort has been made to verify the accuracy of the entries in this book, the
Publishers cannot be held responsible for any errors contained in the work. They would
be glad to receive any information from readers.

WARNING
Some of the stunts and activities in this book are undertaken by experts and should not
be attempted by anyone without adequate training and supervision.

Ripley's Believe It or Not!®

Strikingly True

STRANGE STORIES

www.MasonCrest.com

STRANGE STORIES

Check out these peculiar tales! Learn about

terrifying myths and mind-boggling mysteries.

Discover the photographs of real-life fairies,

the cat that can predict when people are going

to die, and the mysterious giant octopus.

Can you see the ghost in the window? Photographer Kevin Horkin spotted it after he downloaded the image...

strange stories

HeadStand

Kris Sleeman of the Dallas extreme performance group Traumatic Stress Discipline appears to feel no pain. At the grand opening of the Ripley's Believe It or Not! Odditorium in San Antonio, Texas, he lay face down in a pile of freshly broken glass bottles, and then invited Ripley employee Viviana Ray to stand on his head. Kris's pain-defying feats also included having a concrete block on his chest shattered by a sledgehammer while lying on a bed of nails.

FLORIDA MONSTER

Two boys playing on the beach near St. Augustine, Florida, in 1896 spotted the carcass of a huge creature half buried in the sand. It seemed to have a number of tentacles, some up to 30 ft (9 m) long, prompting the belief that it was some kind of giant octopus. However, a similar blob washed up in Chile in 2003 turned out to be a decomposing sperm whale. When some marine creatures decay, their form changes so much that they can look like unidentified sea monsters.

lake monster While fishing 900 ft (275 m) from shore on Russia's 770-sq-mi (1,990-sq-km) Lake Chany in 2010, a man saw his 59-year-old companion hook an unknown creature so powerful that it overturned his boat and dragged him beneath the surface to his death. At least 19 people have vanished on the lake since 2007. Most of the bodies have never been found, but some human corpses have been washed ashore with large bite marks on their bodies. Witnesses have described a snakelike beast with a long neck, a large fin, and a huge tail.

baghdad battery An ancient clay vessel was an early example of a battery—even though batteries were not rediscovered for another 1,800 years. The 2,000-year-old Baghdad Battery contained a copper cylinder and an oxidized iron rod, both held in place by asphalt. When filled with an acid or alkaline liquid, it was capable of producing an electric charge.

metal spheres Over recent decades, miners in Klerksdorp, South Africa, have dug up hundreds of ancient metal spheres that look entirely man-made. However, they were found in Precambrian rock dating back 2.8 billion years—that's over 2.79 billion years before Neanderthal man! The mysterious spheres measure about 1 in (2.5 cm) in diameter and some are etched with three parallel grooves running around the middle.

unique stone The Mystery Stone of Lake Winnipesaukee, New Hampshire, has distinctive markings that make it unique. The egg-shaped stone—found encased in a lump of clay in 1872—has intricate man-made carvings and a hole bored through both ends, but its origins and purpose remain unknown and no matching stones have ever been discovered.

missing belt For reasons unknown, Jupiter loses or regains one of its two belts every ten to 15 years. The planet usually has two dark bands in its atmosphere—one in its northern hemisphere and one in its southern hemisphere—but pictures taken by astronomers in April 2010 showed that the Southern Equatorial Belt had disappeared. The dark belts are clouds created from chemicals such as sulfur and phosphorus, which are blown into bands by 350-mph (560-km/h) winds.

scary site The Borley Rectory in England has been the site of a vast number of mysterious phenomena reported by resident reverends and their families since 1863. The appearance of a ghostly nun, wall writings, stone throwing, windows shattering, bells ringing, unexplained footsteps, a woman becoming locked in a room with no key, and spirit messages tapped out from the frame of a mirror are just some of the incidences said to have occurred. Mediums contacted two spirits there: a French nun murdered on the site and a man who said he would burn down the house. Burn it did—in 1939.

APE MAN

On an expedition to Venezuela in 1920, Swiss geologist François de Loys claimed to have stumbled across a 5-ft-tall (1.5-m), red-haired, tailless ape that walked upright like a human. He shot the animal and photographed it, using a long stick to prop up its head, but the corpse went missing before it could be examined. If genuine, it would have been the first ape ever discovered in the Americas, thereby rewriting the theory of primate evolution, but scientists decided that the photo was merely a common spider monkey whose tail was conveniently hidden or chopped off.

ⓡ RIPLEY RESEARCH

In early July 1947, an object described as a "flying disk" crashed near Roswell, New Mexico. The Roswell Army Air Force (RAAF) insisted the craft was a weather balloon, but speculation mounted that it was a U.F.O. A local rancher saw a shallow trench, several hundred feet long, gouged into the land and recovered metallic debris that turned liquid when dropped. Nurses said they saw small humanoid bodies being examined in a cordoned-off corner of the local hospital. A mortician at a Roswell funeral home revealed he had been asked to provide child-sized, hermetically sealed coffins. To this day no one knows whether the Roswell Incident was a cover-up or a flight of fancy.

Alien Autopsy

A display at the U.F.O. Museum at Roswell, New Mexico, re-creates the alleged autopsy of a dead alien killed when his spacecraft crashed in the area in 1947. The dummy extraterrestrial was originally made for the 1994 movie *Roswell*.

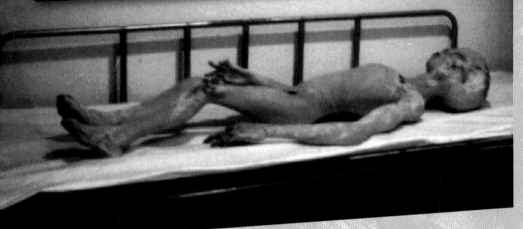

ⓡ fearsome forest Aokigahara Forest, Japan, at the foot of Mount Fuji, is reportedly haunted by strange beasts, monsters, ghosts, and goblins. One popular myth states that the magnetic iron deposits underground cause compasses to malfunction and travelers to get lost in the forest. It is the world's third most popular suicide location.

ⓡ straight line Four ancient historical sites—Easter Island in the Pacific Ocean, the Nazca lines in southern Peru, the Inca city of Ollantaytambo, also in southern Peru, and the Great Pyramid of Giza, Egypt—are all exactly aligned along a straight line. Other world wonders that are within just one-tenth of a degree of this alignment include Persepolis, the capital of ancient Persia; Mohenjo Daro, the ancient capital of the Indus Valley; and the lost city of Petra in modern-day Jordan.

ⓡ ghost ship Carrying a shipment of coal, the *Carroll A. Deering* was found run aground off the coast of North Carolina on January 31, 1921—but its 11-man crew had vanished. There was no sign of the crew's belongings or the ship's navigating instruments, log, or clock, yet evidence in the galley indicated that food was being prepared for the following day's meals.

ⓡ near miss Pilot David Hastings from Norwich, U.K., revealed a close encounter with a U.F.O. when flying over the Mojave Desert in the United States in 1987. He said a mysterious black shape came at his plane head-on, then flashed overhead. Seconds later the object was moving at high speed at the plane's side. Hastings took photos and showed them to U.S. Navy officers, but they refused to comment.

ⓡ band of holes Nearly 7,000 man-made holes are located on a plain near Peru's Pisco Valley—but their origins and purpose remain unknown. The Band of Holes stretches for 1 mi (1.6 km) and some of the holes are up to 7 ft (2.1 m) deep.

ⓡ they're here! A 2010 April Fool's report in a Jordanian newspaper wreaked havoc in one town. Its front-page article described a U.F.O. landing near Jafr, 185 mi (300 km) from Amman. Residents panicked, keeping their children home from school; and Jafr's mayor even sent security forces in search of the aliens. He was at the point of emptying the town of its 13,000 residents when newspaper journalists came clean.

ⓡ aliens welcome Bob Tohak has believed in U.F.O.s since he was a kid. He is so eager to make contact with aliens that he has put a 42-ft-high (13-m) U.F.O. landing port on his property in Poland, Wisconsin. "I'm just hoping that something will show up," he says.

FIRE STARTER

A ghostly young girl was pictured in a building on fire in the town of Wem, England, in 1995. Many were convinced that the photograph captured the ghost of a girl that died after accidentally setting the same building alight in the 17th century. In 2010, after the photographer had died, it was suggested that the 1995 photograph was a fake. The ghostly girl in the fire had been copied from a 1922 Wem postcard, which was spotted in the local newspaper by an eagle-eyed reader.

ⓡ perfect fit The ancient site of Sacsayhuaman, Peru, features three huge stone walls built so expertly that it is impossible to insert a piece of paper between the different-shaped stones, some of which are 9 ft 10 in (3 m) high and weigh 200 tons.

Shocking Stories

ELEPHANT ELECTROCUTION

In an attempt to prove the dangers of Nikola Tesla's alternating current (AC) and the safety of his competing direct current (DC) for use in the home, Thomas Edison electrocuted an elephant in 1903. Topsy was an elephant with Forepaugh Circus at Coney Island's Luna Park, New York City, who had killed three men in three years, and her owners wanted her destroyed. Edison suggested electrocution, a method that had been used for human executions since 1890. Topsy was fed carrots containing potassium cyanide before a current of 6,600 volts was sent through her body, killing her in seconds. A crowd of 1,500 witnessed the event, which Edison also filmed.

MARY, THE HANGED ELEPHANT

Mary was a 5-ton Asian elephant who was hanged for her so-called crimes on September 12, 1916. Her story is a cautionary tale of circus abuse during the early 20th century. She had been prodded behind the ear by her trainer as she bent down to nibble on watermelon rind, so she grabbed him with her trunk and stamped on his head, killing him. Labeled a highly dangerous beast, the public demanded her death. She survived being shot with two dozen rounds, so it was decided to hang her. Mary was hanged by the neck the next day from an industrial crane in Erwin, Tennessee.

phone home A man has spent two years living in a cramped phone booth in Dalian City, Liaoning Province, China. He sleeps by curling up into a ball on top of cushions and hangs his spare clothes from the roof.

elephant collision Driving home from church in Enid, Oklahoma, a couple collided with an elephant that ran across the highway after escaping from a nearby circus. The elephant was unharmed apart from a broken tusk.

quiet companion Alan Derrick of Somerset, England, lived in a house with his friend's dead body hidden behind a sofa from 1998 to 2008.

paid piper Tourism bosses in Vienna, Austria, found a way to frighten off rats from the city's sewers—by playing the bagpipes. The Third Man tours, which walk the sewers made famous by Orson Welles' cult 1949 movie, were closed down when health chiefs ruled that the risk of rat bites was too great, but now they're back in business after hiring a bagpiper whose shrill sounds send the rodents running for cover.

dam coincidence J.G. Tierney drowned in 1922 while surveying the future site of the Hoover Dam. In 1935, his son Patrick became the last person to die in the dam's construction when he fell from an intake tower.

Ashes Live On For $3,000, U.K.-based firm And Vinyly will press a person's ashes or those of their pet into a playable record featuring their favorite music, a personal message, or their last will and testament. The ashes are sprinkled onto a raw piece of vinyl and then pressed by plates. When the plates exert pressure on the vinyl to create the grooves, the ashes are pressed into the record. Customers can also have their own album-cover portrait, created by mixing their ashes into the paint.

political clown A professional clown was elected to represent São Paulo in Congress after picking up 1.3 million votes in the 2010 Brazilian general elections. Tiririca (real name Francisco Oliveira) received the highest number of votes for any federal deputy across the country with his catchy TV slogans including: "What does a federal deputy do? I have no idea, but vote for me and I'll let you know."

traffic calming City transportation officials in Cambridge, Massachusetts, tried to calm drivers annoyed at receiving parking tickets by putting instructions on the reverse side about how to relax by bending the body into simple yoga positions.

fast food Perry Watkins of Buckinghamshire, England, has built a dining table that can travel at speeds of 130 mph (209 km/h). He took the chassis of a Reliant Scimitar sports car, fitted a 4-liter Land Rover Discovery engine boosted by nitrous oxide injection, and then added a table, six dining chairs, and a fake meal. The driver sits under the roast chicken, the tax disc is stuck to a champagne bucket, the tail lights are built into rolled-up napkins, and the exhaust fumes come out of two silver teapots.

ambulance stolen An Illinois man was arrested for stealing an ambulance in Mount Horeb, Wisconsin—with a patient and paramedics still inside it.

bottleneck mystery A 60-mi (96-km) traffic jam trapped thousands of vehicles on the Beijing–Tibet expressway for 11 days in August 2010—but then it completely disappeared overnight without any apparent explanation.

lost letters While on a 2010 field trip to the Alps, Freya Cowan, a geography student from the University of Dundee, Scotland, stumbled across a U.S.-bound mailbag from the *Malabar Princess*, an Air India plane that crashed near the summit of Mont Blanc while en route to London in 1950, killing all 40 passengers and eight crew on board. Some of the correspondence inside the mailbag was still in such good condition that she set about sending 75 letters and birthday cards on to their intended recipients 60 years late.

super sub Cyril Howarth from Lancashire, England, spent $75,000 on converting a 70-ft-long (21-m) canal narrow boat into a replica of a World-War-II German U-boat. Unlike other submarines, this vessel stays strictly on the surface.

Too Close for Comfort Two people found themselves in an unbelievable predicament after being thrown from their motorcycle in Hubei Province, China, in 2010. They flew headfirst into the mouth of a drainpipe just 1 ft 8 in (50 cm) wide and were stuck fast. Fortunately, passersby saw their feet protruding from the polluted water pipe and notified firefighters, who dug the couple free in just ten minutes.

strange stories

Ripley's Believe It or Not!

bullet blocker Colombian tailor Miguel Caballero runs a boutique in Mexico City where jackets and shirts are not stacked by size but by how well they will stop a bullet. He uses secret materials, the most expensive of which, called Black, is so light that it can be scrunched up like paper but will protect the wearer from a bullet fired at point-blank range.

speed of sound Sound travels 4.3 times faster in water than it does in air. When something vibrates, it causes molecules to bump into each other. As water molecules are closer together, the vibrations transfer faster between themselves.

frozen with heat Water can be frozen solid—by applying heat! Supercooled water, which can stay liquid down to −40°F (−40°C), will freeze as it is being heated, as long as the temperature also changes the electrical charge of the surface with which the water is in contact.

black hole Scientists at the Southeast University in Nanjing, China, have created a pocket-size black hole—an 8½-in-wide (21.5-cm) disk that absorbs all the electromagnetic radiation thrown at it. The metal disk has 60 concentric rings that affect the magnetic properties of passing light, bending the beams into the center of the disk and trapping them in a maze of etched grooves.

shrinking coins A powerful electromagnetic field can shrink a coin to half its diameter. The technique is known as high-velocity metal forming, a process which creates an invisible, pulsed magnetic field that batters the coin with a strong shock wave, forcing it to change its physical shape in the blink of an eye.

robot olympics At the 2010 International Robot Olympics held in Harbin, China, humanoid robots from 19 countries competed in 17 disciplines, including running, walking, boxing, kung fu, and dancing. All robots had to be less than 2 ft (60 cm) tall and be built in human form with a head, two arms, and two legs. The opening event, the 5-m (5-yd) sprint, was won in a time of 20 seconds.

ROBOTIC JELLYFISH

Scientists in Germany have developed a range of biologically inspired robotic jellyfish that can swim. The battery-powered jellyfish are propelled through the water by eight electrically driven tentacles, the construction of which is based on the anatomy of fish fins. With the help of sensors and control software, the jellyfish steer themselves and can communicate by means of 11 infrared light-emitting diodes, enabling them to work together as a team and to avoid bumping into each other.

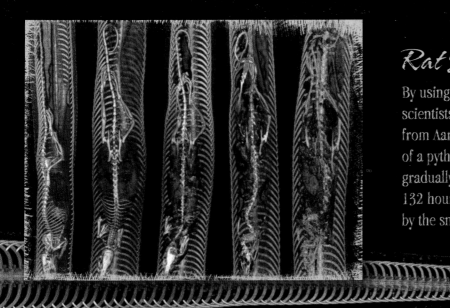

Rat Supper

By using a special scanning technique, scientists Henrik Lauridsen and Kasper Hansen from Aarhus, Denmark, were able to take X-rays of a python digesting a rat. The rat can be seen gradually disappearing during the course of 132 hours—5½ days—after being swallowed by the snake.

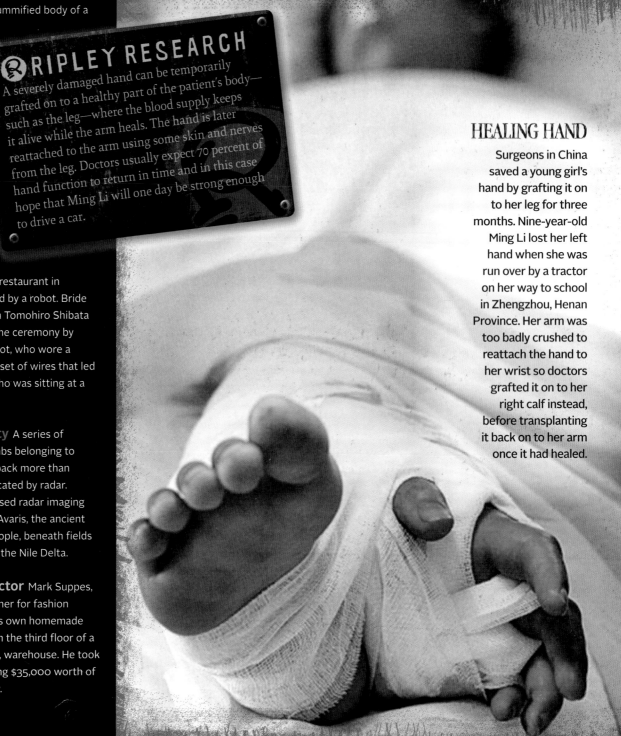

iceman's relatives Nearly 20 years after discovering the mummified body of a 5,300-year-old man—known as Oetzi the iceman—in a melting Alpine glacier, scientists have extracted DNA from a bone in his pelvis with a view to tracking down his living descendants.

robot wedding A wedding that took place in a Tokyo, Japan, restaurant in May 2010 was conducted by a robot. Bride Satoko Inoue and groom Tomohiro Shibata were directed through the ceremony by I-Fairy, a 4-ft (1.2-m) robot, who wore a wreath of flowers and a set of wires that led to a human controller who was sitting at a nearby computer.

underground city A series of streets, houses, and tombs belonging to an Egyptian city dating back more than 3,500 years has been located by radar. Austrian archeologists used radar imaging to show the outlines of Avaris, the ancient capital of the Hyksos people, beneath fields and modern buildings in the Nile Delta.

homemade reactor Mark Suppes, a 32-year-old web designer for fashion house Gucci, has built his own homemade nuclear fusion reactor on the third floor of a Brooklyn, New York City, warehouse. He took two years to build it, using $35,000 worth of parts he bought on eBay.

RIPLEY RESEARCH

A severely damaged hand can be temporarily grafted on to a healthy part of the patient's body—such as the leg—where the blood supply keeps it alive while the arm heals. The hand is later reattached to the arm using some skin and nerves from the leg. Doctors usually expect 70 percent of hand function to return in time and in this case hope that Ming Li will one day be strong enough to drive a car.

HEALING HAND

Surgeons in China saved a young girl's hand by grafting it on to her leg for three months. Nine-year-old Ming Li lost her left hand when she was run over by a tractor on her way to school in Zhengzhou, Henan Province. Her arm was too badly crushed to reattach the hand to her wrist so doctors grafted it on to her right calf instead, before transplanting it back on to her arm once it had healed.

Ripley's Believe It or Not! strange stories

royal residence Janet and Philip Williams have turned their four-bedroom home in Woonona, New South Wales, Australia, into a royal museum, attracting thousands of visitors each year. They have more than 12,000 items of House of Windsor memorabilia, ranging from a life-size model of Queen Elizabeth II to a pair of Prince Charles and Princess Diana slippers. Even the toilet is decorated like a royal throne, complete with purple velvet trim.

$9,000 toothpick In December 2009, a toothpick that once belonged to British author Charles Dickens sold for $9,150 at an auction in New York City.

unwanted coins A stockpile of dollar coins worth more than $1.1 billion is languishing in storage because Americans prefer dollar bills. If stacked, the pile of coins would reach seven times higher than the altitude of the International Space Station.

cow suit Milkman Tony Fowler from Leicestershire, England, wore a black-and-white cow suit to receive his M.B.E. from Queen Elizabeth II at Buckingham Palace in June 2010. The Friesian outfit should have had a tail at the back, but Fowler's dog chewed it off.

same sneakers As part of a bet he made with his Spanish teacher, high-school freshman Ben Hedblom of Tampa, Florida, wore the same pair of sneakers every day for four years until he graduated—even though his toes eventually stuck out the front and he had to encase the shoes in plastic bags on rainy days.

pink lady Los Angeles actress Kitten Kay Sera has worn nothing but pink for over 25 years. "The Pink Lady," as she is known, even wears pink to funerals and once dumped a boyfriend because he was colorblind and therefore unable to appreciate the joy of pink. She dyes her Maltese dog, Kisses, in her favorite color using beetroot juice baths.

manure message To celebrate his wife Carole's 67th birthday, farmer Dick Kleis used a manure spreader to spell out HAP B DAY LUV U in a field visible from the living room of the couple's home in Zwingle, Iowa. It took him three hours and four loads of liquid manure to create the message—he was going to add a heart, too, but he ran out of manure.

bogus tycoon Echoing the real-life escapades of Frank Abagnale Jr. in the movie *Catch Me If You Can*, a 17-year-old boy from Yorkshire, England, posed as an aviation tycoon for six months. He tricked British companies into believing he was about to launch his own airline and that he had a fleet of jets. When the ruse was uncovered, the boy was found to be suffering from a form of autism, which enabled him to recall the exact detail of every airline's flight schedule.

renewed vows Margaret and John Beauvoisin of Hampshire, England, celebrated their diamond wedding anniversary in December 2008 by renewing their vows for the 60th time. The couple got married in 1948 and have renewed their vows every year since 1950, only missing out in 1949 because John was stationed in Bermuda with the Royal Navy.

doll house Bettina Dorfmann from Dusseldorf, Germany, owns more than 6,000 Barbie dolls—and some are worth up to $10,000. An entire room of her house is devoted to displaying 1,500 of them while another 3,000 Barbies from her collection are on show at exhibitions and museums around the world.

just the job Jason Sadler of Ponte Vedra Beach, Florida, earned more than $85,000 in 2009, promoting different businesses by wearing their T-shirts.

reptilian row A row over loud music between two South Carolina motel guests ended with one being accused of slapping the other in the face with the head of a 4-ft (1.2-m) python. The suspect was charged with assault and the weapon—the python—was handed over to his family for safe keeping.

jesus lives When a 50-year-old man was taken to a hospital with minor facial injuries after being hit by a car in Northampton, Massachusetts, in May 2010, he gave his name as Lord Jesus Christ. Police officers checked his I.D. and confirmed that it was indeed his legal name.

family success Father and son Brian and Jared Johnsrud of Marshfield, Wisconsin, both won cricket-spitting contests at the 2009 Central Wisconsin State Fair. Brian spat a thawed cricket 22 ft 8 in (6.9 m) to win the senior title and, minutes later, Jared spat his cricket 10 ft 5 in (3.2 m) to win the 9–11 age division.

DUST BUNNIES

These cuddly looking bunnies are actually composed of household detritus, including Christmas tree needles, discarded toddler toy parts, dryer lint, toenail clippings, and human hair. Suzanne Proulx, from Erie, Pennsylvania, took 2½ years to collect enough dirt and dust to make 16 of her *Dust Bunnies*. Suzanne's first bunnies were a humorous comment on the dust and dirt that seemed to invade her house and multiply like wild rabbits. They are also about rebirth and renewal, taking what has been thrown away and creating something new.

sneaker line Collecting more than 10,500 sneakers sent in by readers, *National Geographic Kids* magazine unveiled a 1.65-mi (2.65-km) line of shoes, tied together by their laces, at Washington, D.C.

house of cards Without using glue or tape, Bryan Berg of Santa Fe, New Mexico, built a model of the Venetian Macao Resort-Hotel in Las Vegas from 218,792 playing cards. It took him 44 days and 4,051 decks of cards to complete the model that measured 33 x 10 ft (10 x 3 m) and weighed 600 lb (272 kg).

great shakes Dorena Young of Wallsburg, Utah, has a collection of more than 3,600 salt-and-pepper shakers. She has been collecting them for more than 60 years and has ones shaped like boats, cats, dogs, deer, vegetables, hats, lighthouses, and sea horses. She even has a pair of J.F.K. and Jackie Onassis salt-and-pepper shakers.

packed court A total of 1,745 students played a single game of dodgeball on the University of California, Irvine, campus in September 2010.

daring plunge Amateur kayaker Christie Glissmeyer from Hood River, Oregon, paddled down the 82-ft-high (25.2-m) Metlako Falls at Eagle Creek, Oregon, in May 2010—a plunge that was nearly twice the height of any waterfall she had previously run.

hairy journey In 2007–08, German adventurer Christoph Rehage walked nearly 2,887 mi (4,646 km) across China from Beijing to Urumqi and took a picture of himself every day to document the growth of his beard.

Lint Leonardo

Laura Bell of Roscommon, Michigan, has made a replica of Leonardo da Vinci's painting *The Last Supper* out of laundry lint that measures 13 ft 8 in x 4 ft 4 in (4 x 1.3 m). She bought towels in the colors she wanted, laundering them separately to achieve the right shades. To obtain the amount of lint she needed to make the picture, she had to do about 800 hours of laundry and it then took her another 200 hours to re-create the famous Renaissance masterpiece.

Ripley's Believe It or Not! strange stories

toy parts Dr. William H. Sewell invented an artificial heart pump prototype with parts from an Erector set toy while at Yale Medical School.

strad beaten In a sound test conducted in Germany before an audience of 180 people, a violin made of wood that had been treated with fungus for nine months was judged better than a $2-million 1711 Stradivarius. Scientists say a fungal attack changes the cell structure of the wood, giving it a warmer, more rounded sound.

lost army Twin brothers Angelo and Alfredo Castiglioni believe they have found the remains of a 50,000-strong Persian army, said to have been drowned in the sands of the Sahara Desert 2,500 years ago. The Italian archeologists have discovered bronze weapons, a silver bracelet, an earring, and hundreds of human bones that are thought to have belonged to the lost army of Persian King Cambyses II, whose men were reportedly buried in a terrible sandstorm in 525 BC.

INVISIBLE MAN

Scientists at Tokyo University have developed camouflage technology that makes people disappear. A coat made of a high-tech reflective material has a video camera placed in it, which sends film to a projector. This, in turn, bounces the moving image off the front of the coat, making the wearer appear transparent, even when the fabric is creased.

stench busters The city of Beijing, China, has installed 100 high-pressure deodorant guns, which can spray dozens of liters of fragrance per minute, to combat the stench from one of the city's many overflowing landfill sites. Beijing's 17 million people generate nearly 20,000 tons of waste every day—7,700 tons more than the capacity of municipal disposal plants.

magnetic lift Scientists have successfully levitated fruit, insects, frogs, and mice by applying a repelling effect on the water molecules in their bodies with powerful magnets.

quake-proof bed Wang Wenxi from Shijiazhuang, China, has invented an earthquake-proof bed. When an earthquake strikes, a strong board automatically slides into place, protecting the person from falling debris. His secure bed has cupboards at both ends with water, canned food, a hammer, and a megaphone to help the occupant survive for several days beneath rubble.

solar slug *Elysia chlorotica*, a green sea slug that lives along the Atlantic seaboard of the United States, runs on solar power. Scientists at the University of Maine have discovered that it photosynthesizes using genes "stolen" from the algae it eats.

MAGIC GEL

"Aerogel" was created in 1931 by U.S. scientist Samuel Stephens Kistler following a bet with a colleague over who could replace the liquid in gel with a gas without causing shrinkage. Even though it is 99.8 percent air, the unique substance aerogel can withstand temperatures of up to 2,550°F (1,400°C) and is strong enough to support 2,000 times its own weight.

green

RIPLEY RESEARCH

Aerogel is derived from a silica gel, the liquid component of which is replaced with a gas to create an extremely low-density solid. It is 1,000 times less dense than glass, making it very lightweight. It has been used by NASA for thermal insulation of space suits and on the Mars Rover vehicle on its Stardust Mission to trap space dust. Whereas cosmic dust vaporizes on impact with solids and passes through gas, the nature of aerogel allows it to trap particles traveling at 1,350 mph (2,170 km/h) without damaging them.

Solar Detector

The Super-Kamiokande Detector is a gigantic cylindrical stainless steel tank, measuring 136 ft (41 m) high and 129 ft (39 m) in diameter, located more than half a mile underground in Japan. Holding 50,000 tons of water, it is lined with 11,146 ultra-sensitive light detectors and serves as a scientific observatory to monitor solar neutrinos—particles that are produced in the Sun by nuclear fusion. This will help us understand what goes on inside the Sun and how matter was created in the early Universe. The Detector is located underground to shield the experiments from cosmic rays and background radiation.

WEE FOLK

Two tree pods shaped like fairies are kept in a glass box at the Wat Phrapangmuni Temple near Sing Buri, Thailand. According to popular belief, these *Naree Pons* (or pod people) appeared to the Buddha as beautiful women while he meditated in a secluded area. They then vanished and left behind a miniature humanoid pod form on a nearby tree.

advanced mechanism When the Antikythera Mechanism was recovered from a shipwreck near Crete in 1900, the writing on its case indicated that it was made around 80 BC—but an X-ray revealed a system of differential gears not known to have existed until AD 1575. It is believed to be an ancient mechanical computer designed to calculate astronomical positions, but its sophistication is in fact comparable to a 19th-century Swiss clock.

stone balls In the Costa Rican jungle in the 1930s, workmen found over 300 man-made stone balls, many perfectly spherical and varying in size from as small as a tennis ball to huge boulders 8 ft (2.4 m) in diameter and weighing 15 tons. The stones date back at least 500 years, but nobody knows who made them and how such spherical precision was achieved.

flaming fireball A massive fireball lit up the sky over five U.S. states—Missouri, Iowa, Wisconsin, Illinois, and Indiana—on the night of April 14, 2010. Puzzled scientists say it could have been a meteor, a chunk from an asteroid, or rocket debris.

milk miracle For several hours on September 21, 1995, Hindu religious statues all over the world drank milk. When a worshiper at a temple in New Delhi, India, offered a spoonful of milk to the trunk of a statue of the elephant-headed deity Ganesha, the liquid was seen to disappear. Soon Hindu temples in the U.K., Canada, Dubai, and Nepal were reporting similar occurrences. Scientists were baffled by the phenomenon, which stopped before the end of the day when statues suddenly refused to accept milk.

unfinished city Having spent years constructing 30-ft-high (9-m) walls from perfectly hewn basalt, the inhabitants of the ancient city of Nan Madol, in the Micronesia region of the Pacific, mysteriously abandoned it, leaving some of the walls unfinished.

who goes hare! In 1971, a rabbit was shot by Jasper Barrett near his home in Jefferson, South Carolina. On being prepared for the pot by his wife and a friend, the outline in black of a woman's face was found on the skinned flesh of one foreleg. It was about an inch across and had a rosebud mouth, curly hair, and long lashes. Within a week of the news breaking, 4,000 people had trekked to see the face and extra police were called in to control the crowds.

GHOSTLY VISION

When Kevin Horkin downloaded this photo and saw a pale young woman peering from a window on the first floor of Gwrych Castle in Abergele, he knew something spooky was afoot. The huge Welsh castle has been derelict since 1985 and the floor crumbled away years ago, so no one could possibly have been standing there. Countless sightings, orbs, cold spots, and cases of objects moving have been recorded at Gwrych, said to be the most haunted building in Wales.

ghostly pleas Sightings of the ghosts of tormented slaves from the 1830s have been reported at Lalaurie House, New Orleans. Servants who begged the assistance of outsiders when the house was burning are seen running back inside, slamming doors, shouting repeatedly. Several people have seen ghostly faces of the dead peering from upper windows.

eerie face The image of a child's face dating back over 100 years was found burned onto an old oven door at a restaurant in Saint John, New Brunswick, Canada, in the 1980s. A lady visitor to the property at 31 Leinster Street had gone into the cellar to inspect the original brick oven, but when the dirt was cleaned away the smiling face of a young girl became visible in the iron door. It is believed the family living there in the late 19th century had used the oven as a crematorium to dispose of their dead daughter. The image on the door was caused by carbons given off by the body during burning, the bright light of the fire having acted as a lens.

Burning Mystery

When 92-year-old Dr. John Irving Bentley was found in the bathroom of his home in Coudersport, Pennsylvania, in December 1966, all that remained of him was a pile of ashes and the lower half of his right leg. He is thought to have been a victim of spontaneous human combustion, a phenomenon where people suddenly burst into flames for no apparent reason. Although almost his entire body had been consumed by an intense heat, the fire was confined to a small area and, apart from a hole in the floor where he had been standing, the rest of the room was largely undamaged. The rubber tips on his walking frame were still intact and a nearby bathtub was hardly scorched.

ⓡ auto inferno Jeanna Winchester was riding in a car with a friend in Jacksonville, Florida, in 1980 when she was mysteriously engulfed in bright yellow flames. There was no spilled gas, she had not been smoking, and the car window was up. Jeanna survived, although she suffered severe burns. The car interior, however, was virtually undamaged, with just a slight browning on Jeanna's white leather seat.

ⓡ charred remains In March 1997, the charred remains of 76-year-old John O'Connor were found in a chair some distance from the hearth of his living room in County Kerry, Ireland. Only his head, upper torso, and feet remained unburned, yet there was little smoke damage to the room or the furniture.

ⓡ burning dress A dress being worn by Mrs. Charles Williamson of Bladenboro, North Carolina, unaccountably burst into flames in 1932. Her husband and daughter ripped off the blazing dress with their bare hands yet none of the three suffered any burns. Over the next four days, various items in the house suddenly caught fire, but each time the flames, which had neither smoke nor smell, simply vanished after the article had burned itself out.

ⓡ fatal fire Mrs. Olga Worth Stephens, 75, of Dallas, Texas, suddenly burst into flames while waiting in her parked car in 1964 and died before anyone could rescue her. The car was undamaged and firemen concluded that nothing in the vehicle could have started the fatal blaze.

ⓡ paper puzzle Anna Martin of West Philadelphia, Pennsylvania, was found incinerated at home in 1957, her body totally consumed by fire except for a piece of her torso and her shoes. The medical examiner estimated that temperatures must have reached at least 1,700°F (925°C)—far too hot for anything in the room to remain uncharred, yet newspapers lying just 2 ft (60 cm) away were found intact.

ⓡ vaporized flesh At Blackwood, Wales, in 1980, a man's body was found burned beyond recognition in his living room. The armchair that he was sitting in was hardly damaged—neither were some plastic objects nearby—but the fire was so intense that it left a coating of vaporized flesh on the ceiling.

Ripley's Believe It or Not!

strange stories

blamed vampire A Fruita, Colorado, woman who drove her car into a canal in June 2010 blamed the accident on a vampire. She said she was driving on a dirt road late at night, when she spotted a vampire in the middle of the road and hastily put the car in reverse. When troopers arrived, they found the woman's car in the canal but there was no sign of the vampire.

upside down Wang Xiaoyu, a barber from Changsha, Hunan Province, China, gives haircuts while standing on his head. A trained martial artist, he performs his headstands on a table to achieve the right height for cutting customers' hair.

leisurely stroll Paul Railton was fined $100 in 2010 for taking his dog for a walk while driving alongside in his car. He was spotted driving at low speed along a country lane in County Durham, England, holding his Lurcher's leash through the car window as the dog trotted next to him.

CAR COFFINS

Automobile fan Danny Mendez of Winchester, California, has designed a range of $1,500 fiberglass coffins in the shapes of classic cars. Each Cruisin' Casket features motorcycle headlights, alloy wheels from golf carts, and extending side exhausts that serve as handles for pallbearers. In the absence of a death in the family, the coffins can also double as ice coolers.

sailing in circles A nautical novice who thought he was sailing around the coast of Britain in a counterclockwise direction ended up circling a small island off Kent instead. He was rescued by a lifeboat after running out of fuel off the 8-mi-wide (13-km) Isle of Sheppey, whose shore he had been hugging day and night on the principle of keeping the land to his right. He had not realized that Sheppey was an island.

mayo misery A consignment of mayonnaise fell off the back of a truck in Hyogo, Japan, causing an eight-vehicle pileup as cars and motorcycles skidded wildly on the crushed sauce. The highway had to be closed for five hours.

subway pushers Human "pushers" are hired to work on Tokyo's subway system to help cram more people into the overcrowded train cars.

wake up! An Australian mining company has invented a hat that wakes up sleepy truck drivers. The hi-tech SmartCap is fitted with brain monitoring sensors, and if the driver seems to be drifting off, the cap sends a message to a computer screen in the truck cab, which then flashes a warning.

road hogs A section of road near Eureka, Missouri, is covered with asphalt made from recycled pig manure, courtesy of a nearby hog farm.

concrete breaker Kung fu champion Chris Roper from Suffolk, England, can break a 26-in-thick (66-cm) block of concrete with his foot, 20 in (51 cm) with his elbow, and 12 in (30 cm) with his bare hand.

strong hair In November 2009, Manjit Singh from Leicester, England, pulled a double-decker London bus 70 ft (21 m)—using only his hair. By attaching a clamp to his thick ponytail, he managed to pull the seven-ton bus through Battersea Park. The feat made up for his disappointment in 2007, when he had been unable to pull a similar bus with his ears.

versatile performer Yang Guanghe, from China's Guizhou Province, can perform more than 30 different stunts—including standing on lit lightbulbs, lifting buckets of water with his eyelids, using an electric drill on his nose, standing on upturned knives, pulling a car with his eyelids, and inserting a live snake into one of his nostrils then pulling it out from his mouth.

facebook phenomenon People across the world spend more than 700 billion minutes a month surfing through the website of Facebook, the Palo Alto, California-based social networking site. Since it was launched in 2004, more than 500 million people have joined Facebook—that's around eight percent of the world's population.

GUARDIAN ANGEL

Police in Fribourg, Switzerland, hired a roadside angel to stop motorists driving too fast. Dressed all in white, the angel, played by a bearded actor, stood at different locations and flapped his wings at speeding drivers.

strong stomach Julika Faciu from Piatra Neamt, Romania, allowed 50 motorbikes and a 3-ton jeep to ride over his stomach, one by one.

google alert A ten-year-old girl who decided to act dead while playing in the street with her friends sparked panic among neighbors when her image was captured by Google Street View cameras. Azura Beebeejaun was pictured lying face down on the pavement outside her home in Worcester, England, prompting residents browsing their neighborhood online to fear they had stumbled across a murder scene.

junior matador At age 12 and standing only 4 ft 10 in (1.5 m) tall, seventh-grader Michel Lagravere from Mérida, Mexico, is a seasoned bullfighter who has challenged more than 50 snorting, charging 500-lb (227-kg) beasts in Colombia, Peru, and France, as well as in his native country. Known as "Michelito," he first stepped into the ring with a young bull when he was just four and a half years old.

clean teen As a teenager, James Brown from Nottinghamshire, England, had a collection of 50 vacuum cleaners—and his love for them has led to him opening Britain's first vacuum cleaner museum. He can identify different brands of vacuum cleaners in his collection simply by their sound.

STRONG MAN

George Lavasseur, a strong man with Ringling Bros Circus in the early 20th century, was able to bear a 17-man human pyramid on his back that weighed a total of 3,257 lb (1,477 kg). The Detroit-born performer could also carry the weight of a fully grown elephant.

3257 LBS

Ripley's Believe It or Not!®

king charles Charles Wesley Mumbere worked as a nurses' aide for years in the United States, but on October 19, 2009, he reclaimed his crown as head of the mountainous kingdom of Rwenzururu in Uganda, ruling over about 300,000 people.

skateboarding priest Reverend Zoltan Lendvai, a Hungarian Catholic priest, spreads the word of God from his skateboard. Father Lendvai, whose first skateboard incorporated the papal coat of arms, has become a YouTube hit with a video showing the 45-year-old, in full clerical dress, demonstrating his moves for youngsters outside his church in Redics. He believes his skateboarding prowess will encourage more young people to attend church.

rolling, rolling, rolling... Lotan Baba, the "Rolling Saint" of India, spreads his message of peace by rolling on the ground from town to town across the country. He rolls 6–8 mi (10–12 km) a day and estimates that over the years he has rolled about 18,650 mi (30,000 km). His enthusiasm for rolling may be partly explained by the fact that as penance he once spent seven years standing upright, in the same place.

vertical burials An Australian funeral home is saving space by burying people vertically. Melbourne company Upright Burials places each corpse in a biodegradable bag and then lowers the body feet first into a cylindrical hole about 30 in (75 cm) in diameter and 9½ ft (3 m) deep. Using this method, the company hopes to bury up to 40,000 bodies in a field outside the city.

debt unpaid Former British Prime Minister Winston Churchill (1874–1965) died owing 13 rupees to the Bangalore Club of Bangalore, India. The club has maintained the ledger showing that debt and displays it—but refuses to allow anyone to pay his tab.

idaho caveman Richard "Dugout Dick" Zimmerman (1916–2010) left his old life as a farmhand behind in 1947 and began digging out a series of caves near Salmon, Idaho. He cultivated a garden and lived without modern amenities for more than 60 years. Some of his caves were up to 60 ft (18.5 m) deep and were furnished with cast-off doors, car windows, old tires, and other discarded items.

homemade plane In July 2010, 82-year-old Arnold Ebneter of Woodinville, Washington State, flew his homemade lightweight airplane, the E-1, nonstop from Everett, Washington State, to Fredericksburg, Virginia—a journey of 2,327 mi (3,746 km)—in 18 hours 27 minutes.

in a flap When Darren Cubberly's racing pigeon, Houdini, failed to arrive at the end of a 224-mi (360-km), six-hour race from the island of Guernsey to the West Midlands, England, he gave up hope of seeing the bird again. Then, five weeks later he received a call from Panama City—5,200 mi (8,370 km) away—to say that Houdini was there. It is thought she landed on a ship traveling to the area.

fire trim Italian-American hairdresser Pietro Santoro cuts hair using a naked flame at his barber shop in Washington, D.C. He says that cutting hair with fire gives it more body.

Dried Shark

A seafront store in Taiwan offers whole dried sharks for sale at a price of 6,500 Hong Kong dollars (U.S.$844) per 1 lb 5 oz (600 g). Shark fins are a popular delicacy in Chinese soup, while other parts of the shark are considered to have beneficial medicinal properties.

SKELETON STAFF

When the Post-Mortem Club held its annual breakfast in Chicago in 1934, the guest of honor was the skeleton of its late founder, Mr. J. M. McAdou of Florida, who had died the previous year. The club was an organization of naprapaths (practitioners of a manual medical technique similar to osteopathy) and had a rule that stated each member should leave them his skeleton so that it could attend future meetings...although probably not vote.

polar riddle When video footage showed a large, white beast lying on the shore, British TV presenter Naomi Lloyd excitedly told viewers that a polar bear from the Arctic had been washed up in Bude, Cornwall. It subsequently emerged that the animal was actually a cow that had been bleached white by seawater.

game proposal A New York City video-game fan proposed to his girlfriend with gold coins in a specially designed level of Super Mario World. Having persuaded her to play the game, he used a level-editing program called Lunar Magic to spell out "Lisa will you marry me?" on screen. He then recorded her delighted reaction in a video posted on YouTube.

resuscitating roadkill A 55-year-old man was arrested on a remote highway northeast of Pittsburgh, Pennsylvania, after he was seen performing mouth-to-mouth resuscitation on roadkill. Witnesses said the possum in question was not just playing dead, it had been deceased for some time.

slimy cure According to the African religion of *Ifa Orisha*, drinking the juices and mucus of Giant African snails can cure the sick.

dog driver A man was run over by his own dog in 2010 after it jumped into his pickup truck and accidentally knocked it into gear. Christopher Bishop of Webster, Florida, was lying under his truck checking for oil leaks and had the vehicle in neutral, the engine running, and the driver's door open, when his bulldog, Tassey, leaped in and hit the gear stick into reverse, sending the vehicle rolling over his owner's body. Luckily, Christopher survived the incident without major injury.

RIPLEY'S HERO

Daring Thai snake charmer Khum Chaibuddee, also known as the "King of Cobras," was honored as a Ripley's Ambassador by the *Ripley's Believe It or Not* museum in Pattaya, Thailand, in 2010. He celebrated by performing with his deadly cobras and even kissing them, his signature trick. In *Ripley's Believe It or Not! The Remarkable Revealed*, we reported that a fearless Khum had kissed 19 highly poisonous cobras one by one on the head without being bitten.

raining birds
More than 5,000 dead red-winged blackbirds rained from the sky over Beebe, Arkansas, on January 1, 2011, littering the streets with corpses. Three days later, another 500 birds—dead or dying—fell onto the Louisiana Highway in Pointe Coupee Parish. Scientists say the birds, disturbed by New Year's Eve fireworks or a passing train, may have died after flying at night and crashing into trees, houses, and power lines.

marfa lights
For over a century, witnesses have been spooked by the Marfa Lights, a strange light phenomenon occurring around the Mitchell Flats, outside Marfa, Texas. Descriptions range from small dancing lights in the sky to a single, stationary bright light that changes color. In a failed attempt to solve the mystery, a former World-War-II pilot even chased the lights in an airplane.

tunguska explosion
At 7.14 a.m. on June 30, 1908, a mysterious explosion took place in central Siberia that was 1,000 times more powerful than the atomic bombs dropped on the Japanese cities of Hiroshima and Nagasaki in 1945. The Tunguska Explosion leveled a staggering 80 million trees over an area of 830 sq mi (2,150 sq m) and generated a huge shock wave that knocked people to the ground 37 mi (60 km) from the epicenter. Experts believe it could have been caused by a meteorite crashing into the Earth.

FLOATING HEADS
This may look like the disembodied head of Alfred Hitchcock floating in a field, but it is actually the eerie work of Spanish artist Ibon Mainar. Ibon uses ingenious projector techniques to beam images of famous people or objects, such as chandeliers and spooky cats' eyes, onto natural settings around his home in San Sebastián, Spain. He employs a car-mounted unit to project the images onto water, trees, and mountainsides, and when viewed in real life the pictures have a strangely lifelike 3-D effect.

tunnel network
Ten large holes and a network of tunnels—some big enough for a person to stand up in—suddenly appeared in the ground in the Krasnoyarsk region of Siberia in 2006. It is thought they were either the work of unknown animals or were somehow related to an earthquake that had hit the area in 2003.

ghost yacht
A 40-ft-long (12-m) yacht, the *Kaz II*, was found drifting off the coast of Queensland, Australia, in 2007, with its engine running and a table laid for dinner but no sign of its three-man crew. The radio was working, the computers were running, and the lifejackets were still on board, but there was no evidence of foul play and no bodies were ever found.

yellow deposit
An unexplained greenish-yellow goo fell from the skies and splattered houses and streets in Snyder, New York State, on January 18, 2011. As temperatures dropped, homes were coated in yellow or green icicles.

taos hum
For years, people in and around the town of Taos, New Mexico, have been able to hear a curious low-frequency noise known as the Taos Hum. Not audible to everyone, it has been described as sounding like a distant diesel engine, but its source has never been traced.

desert mummies
Excavations at a 4,000-year-old graveyard in China's remote Taklimakan Desert uncovered around 200 mummies—but their D.N.A. showed they had partly European ancestry. The mummies also had European features, such as long noses, high cheekbones, and reddish-blond hair.

SOMETHING IN THE GARDEN
Phyllis Bacon believes a fairy fluttered into her life and out again one evening in her garden in London, England. She wasn't even looking through the camera when she held it at arm's length and clicked the button to take a picture of her backyard. She spent months scouring the Internet for butterflies, beetles, and moths that might match the image, but came up with nothing.

Real Fairies?

As reported in *Ripley's Believe It or Not! Enter If You Dare*, two cousins, Frances Griffiths and Elsie Wright, rocked the world in 1917 when they said they had photographed fairies in a leafy glen near Elsie's home in Cottingley, England. The five photographs were highly convincing and were published by Arthur Conan Doyle, author of the Sherlock Holmes novels, with an accompanying article. Many experts in photography and psychic research, who examined the pictures and questioned the girls, came to the conclusion that the images were genuine. It was only in the 1980s the girls admitted to faking the pictures with cardboard cutouts and hatpins. However, when Frances Griffiths' daughter appeared on the BBC TV show *The Antiques Roadshow* on January 4, 2009, with a camera given to her by Conan Doyle, she revealed that her mother claimed right up to her death that the fifth and final photograph, taken on a separate occasion and shown here, was genuine.

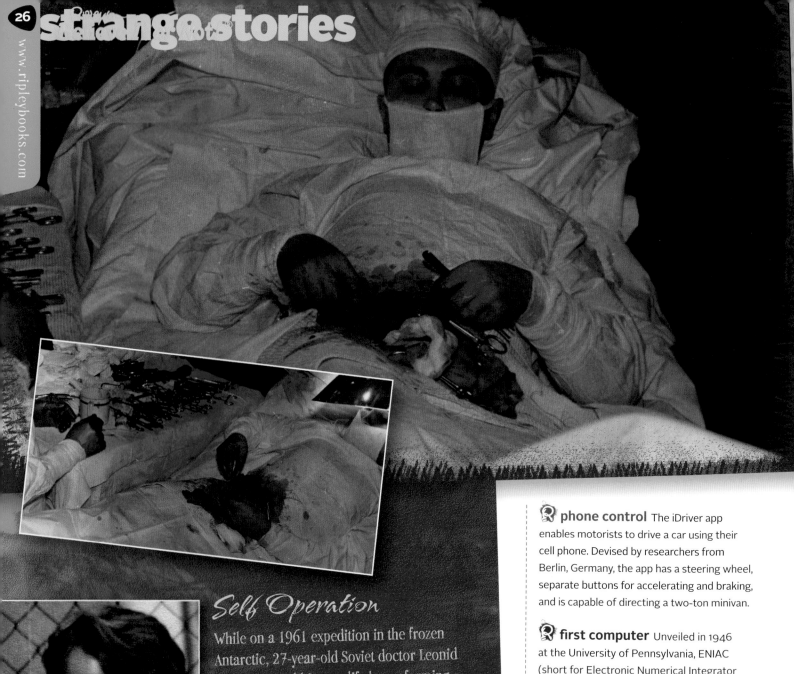

Self Operation

While on a 1961 expedition in the frozen Antarctic, 27-year-old Soviet doctor Leonid Rogozov saved his own life by performing an operation on himself to remove his dangerously inflamed appendix.

Suffering from fever and a pain in his right lower belly, he quickly diagnosed appendicitis. However, he knew that no aid plane would be able to cope with the blizzards or reach such a remote spot in time to evacuate him, so, as the only doctor at the station, he set about conducting an auto-appendectomy on the night of April 30. He was assisted by an engineer and the station's meteorologist, who handed him the medical instruments and held a small mirror at his belly to help him see what he was doing.

After administering a local anesthetic of novocaine solution, Rogozov made a 4¾-in (12-cm) incision in his lower abdomen with a scalpel. Working without gloves and guiding himself mainly by touch from a semi-reclining position, he proceeded to remove the appendix before injecting antibiotic into the abdominal cavity and closing the wound. The self-operation took 1 hour 45 minutes, and saved his life. If he had left it another day his appendix would have burst. His stitches were taken out a week later and he made a complete recovery.

phone control The iDriver app enables motorists to drive a car using their cell phone. Devised by researchers from Berlin, Germany, the app has a steering wheel, separate buttons for accelerating and braking, and is capable of directing a two-ton minivan.

first computer Unveiled in 1946 at the University of Pennsylvania, ENIAC (short for Electronic Numerical Integrator and Computer) was the world's first general-purpose computer. It weighed 30 tons and occupied an entire room. Yet its computing ability can be re-created today on a silicon chip smaller than your thumbnail.

anti-flu suit A Japanese menswear company has developed a suit that it claims protects the wearer from the deadly H1N1 strain of influenza. The $550 suit, produced by the Haruyama Trading Company, is coated with the chemical titanium dioxide—an ingredient of toothpaste and cosmetics—that reacts to light to break down and kill the virus on contact.

oh, crumbs! The Swiss-based Large Hadron Collider, the world's most powerful particle accelerator and probably the most complex machine ever built, was shut down in 2009 after a bird passing overhead dropped a piece of bread on a section of machinery, causing parts of the accelerator to overheat.

skiing robot A skiing robot that can navigate slalom courses has been developed by researchers at the Jozef Stefan Institute in Slovenia. The robot, which is about the size of an eight-year-old child and uses regular skis, has a pair of computer systems. One of them is attached to cameras to help plot the robot's course down the slope, the other is attached to gyroscopes and force sensors to keep it stable.

beige world After examining the amounts of light emitted by galaxies, scientists at NASA have concluded that the Universe is not really black at all—more a dull beige. They say that the shade is constantly changing and has become much less blue over the past ten billion years because redder stars are now more dominant.

large dish The Large Zenith Telescope at the University of British Columbia in Canada uses a mirror made from a spinning dish of liquid mercury nearly 20 ft (6.1 m) in diameter.

bell tribute On August 4, 1922—the day of the funeral of Alexander Graham Bell—all telephone services in the United States and Canada were shut down for one minute as a tribute to the inventor, who, in the 1870s, had invented the first workable telephone.

plasma knife To help stem the loss of blood from serious wounds, the U.S. military has been testing a plasma knife, with a blade consisting of heated, ionized gas, which can cut through flesh just as easily as a steel scalpel. The plasma knife seals off the damaged flesh, stopping the bleeding and protecting against infection.

stone-age surgery When archeologists in France unearthed the 7,000-year-old skeleton of a man, they were amazed to see that he had an amputated arm. The Stone Age surgery was probably performed using a sharpened flint stone, with painkilling plants acting as an anesthetic, and an antiseptic herb such as sage being used to clean the wound.

rotten eggs As part of a safety campaign in 2010, Puget Sound Energy, a utility company in Washington State, added the stench of rotten eggs to its gas bills. Natural gas is odorless, but providers add a chemical with a sulfurlike aroma to the gas so that leaks can be detected.

BODY ART

Hong Kong radiologist Kai-Hung Fung has created stunning images of the human body that look like works of art. Dr. Fung scans the patient using a conventional computer topography (CT) scan, generally used for diagnosing brain and cardiac problems, before feeding the information into a computer and adding vivid color.

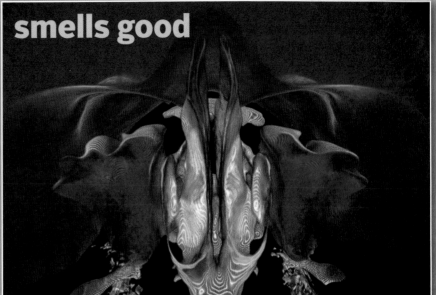

smells good

A view behind the human nose

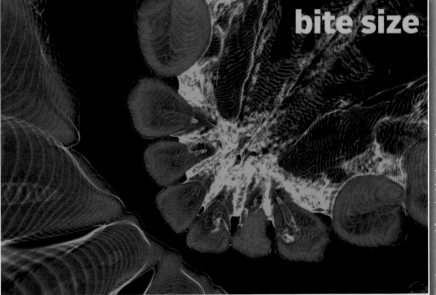

bite size

Teeth captured from inside the mouth

say what?

Curves inside an ear

strange stories

Ⓡ **flamboyant funeral** Flamboyant Hong-Kong lawyer Kai-bong Chau, 75, was buried in March 2010 with paper replicas of his gold and pink Rolls-Royce cars and a selection of his most colorful outfits. Paper models of cars, homes, and money are traditionally burned at Chinese funerals to provide the dead with comfort and luxuries in the afterlife.

Ⓡ **strange venue** Jason and Rachael Storm decided to start their life together in 2008 by getting married at a place where it usually comes to an end—a funeral home in St. Joseph Township, Michigan, where the groom was a director.

CRAB DISPENSER

A food vending machine in Nanjing, China, sells live crabs. Designed by Shi Tuanjie, the machine offers live hairy crabs and accompanying bottles of vinegar. The crustaceans vary in price from $2 to $7, according to size. The crabs, a tasty delicacy in the region, are packed into plastic boxes and chilled to 40°F (5°C), leaving them sedated but still alive. An average of 200 crabs a day are sold, and customers are promised compensation of three live crabs should their purchase happen to be dead.

Ⓡ **favorite ride** Vic Kleman of Knoxville, Pennsylvania, has ridden the Jack Rabbit roller coaster at Kennywood Park in West Mifflin more than 4,700 times since 1959. To celebrate the 90th birthday of the wooden ride, which has an 85-ft (26-m) double-dip drop, 78-year-old Vic went on it 90 times in one day in August 2010. He celebrated his 80th birthday in 2012 by going on the ride again, 80 times in a row.

Ⓡ **wrong funeral** After reading a death notice in her local paper in Merthyr Tydfil, Wales, stating that upholsterer Ron Jones had passed away, Margaret Griffiths sat through the funeral service for her old friend—only to discover later that she had got the wrong Ron Jones. The confusion arose because there were two men named Ron Jones of similar age in the town and both had worked as upholsterers.

Ⓡ **young undertaker** In September 2010, George Simnett set up his own funeral business in Leicestershire, England—at age 17.

Ⓡ **snow palace** To create a fairy-tale setting for his ultimately successful marriage proposal to Christi Lombardo in February 2010, Ryan Knotek built a snow castle near his home in Parma, Ohio. Using blocks of snow, he constructed a one-room, one-story palace topped with roof spires and furnished inside with a portable heater to keep the winter chill away.

Ⓡ **blessed computers** To attract bankers and financiers from the City of London to his church, the Rev. Canon David Parrott performed a service in which he blessed their cell phones and laptop computers.

Ⓡ **mobile chapel** A 1942 firetruck owned by Rev. Darrell Best, of Shelbyville, Illinois, has been converted into a mobile wedding chapel called "Best Man." It has stained glass windows, an altar, two wooden pews, and a fully working pipe organ.

Ⓡ **bmw tomb** Following his death at age 51, the family of motoring fanatic Steve Marsh of London, England, built him a tomb in the shape of a shiny black BMW, complete with personalized number plate "STEVE 1" and a parking ticket.

Ⓡ **boxed art** Vending machines in Germany sell miniature works of art in boxes for less than $3. About 100 refurbished machines, which once sold cigarettes or chewing gum, now sell tiny one-off sculptures, collages, and paintings by professional artists.

Ⓡ **saddle sore** Riding 49cc mini-bikes that averaged just 20 mph (32 km/h), Ryan Galbraith and Chris Stinson traveled the 445 mi (716 km) from Denver, Colorado, to Sturgis, South Dakota, in 25 hours 29 minutes in 2009.

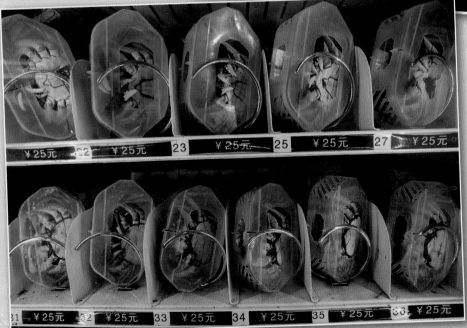

high fives Paralympic Alpine skiing silver medalist Josh Dueck of Vernon, Canada, high-fived 9,307 people in 24 hours in Vancouver in September 2010.

pole balance David Cain of Liberty Township, Ohio, can balance a 58-ft-long (17.7-m) fiberglass pole on his chin for more than 21 seconds. It took him two years to master the skill.

Huge Hole

A 66-ft-wide (20-m) sinkhole opened up overnight in the yard of the Zhang family home in Leshan, China. Several fruit trees disappeared down the hole, which was more than 130 ft (40 m) deep and stopped less than 3 ft (1 m) from the house.

filthy rich Sixty-year-old Curt Degerman of Skellefteå, Sweden, ate from trash bins and collected cans for recycling for 40 years, but when he died it was discovered he was worth more than $1.4 million.

loop the loops Setting off at an altitude of 5,900 ft (1,800 m), Hungarian tandem paraglider Pál Takáts and his co-pilot Gábor Kézi performed 45 consecutive loop the loops on their descent over Lake Walenstadt, Switzerland.

wayward gps In 2009, a driver was fined after following the directions of his GPS up a narrow dirt track, unsuitable for cars, to the very edge of a 100-ft (30-m) cliff drop in West Yorkshire, England.

welded to flagpole On April 29, 2009, Alex Almy and Jesse Poe, seniors at Fruita Monument High School in Fruita, Colorado, spent 75 minutes welding a car around their school's flagpole as a year-end prank. They took off the passenger door and part of the roof to slide the Eagle hatchback into place before getting busy with welding tools. However, because the flagpole itself was undamaged and the boys agreed to remove the car, no one was punished.

strange stories

Ripley's
Believe It or Not!

Ectoplasm

Communicating with the dead was a popular pursuit in the early 20th century, and mediums who went into a trancelike state were often seen to produce a peculiar white substance called ectoplasm from their mouth, ears, nose, or navel. Participants at seances would then watch in amazement as the ectoplasm was apparently transformed into spiritual faces, fully functional arms, and even entire bodies. It also appeared to give mediums the power to perform astonishing feats of telekinesis, such as raising tables and chairs without any physical contact. But was it all genuine or just an elaborate hoax?

GHOSTLY FACE

At a 1912 seance, ectoplasm from French medium Eva C. (Eva Carrière) formed into the shape of a man's head, which, according to an observer, then made bowing movements. Eva C. was renowned for being able to produce ectoplasm, but skeptics said it was nothing more than chewed paper or fabric that had been regurgitated. Once, after the flow of ectoplasm had been reabsorbed into her mouth, she was given a powerful emetic and when she failed to vomit, the doubters were satisfied that she had not swallowed anything to fake the ectoplasm.

RIPLEY RESEARCH

Ectoplasm is the supposed residue left by ghostly spirits. The term was first used in 1894 by French scientist Charles Richet to explain a third arm that seemed to grow from Italian medium Eusapia Palladino. Ectoplasm was described as having a rubbery texture with a smell of ozone. Touching it or exposing it to light was said to cause injury to mediums, which was why they insisted on conducting seances in the dark. Skeptics said this was simply to hide their deception and indeed many mediums were caught creating their own fake ectoplasm by using thin strips of muslin, egg white, soap, or paper. However, other respected witnesses maintained that ectoplasm moved as if it were genuinely alive and could change its shape at will.

mockbeggar coffins
In the early 20th century, a number of wooden coffins—containing the remains of men, women, and children—were discovered buried in mud at Mockbeggar, Newfoundland, Canada. The wood was not local, leading to speculation that the deceased could have been French fishermen, but the French did not usually take their families when they went fishing in the area. To this day, their identities remain a mystery.

body glow
In 1934, Anna Monaro, an asthma patient at a hospital in Pirano, Italy, produced a flickering glow of blue light from her chest for up to 10 seconds at a time while she was asleep. Observed by doctors, scientists, and government officials, the phenomenon occurred a number of times each night until it suddenly stopped several weeks later. Physicians suggested the glow might have been caused by certain compounds in the woman's skin.

ringing rocks
Ringing Rocks Park in Upper Black Eddy, Pennsylvania, is home to a field of boulders, which, when hit with a solid object such as a hammer, produce melodious bell-like tones.

fish deaths
In December 2010, more than 80,000 drum fish were found dead along a 20-mile (32-km) stretch of the Arkansas River and 10,000 red drum fish were mysteriously washed up dead in Chesapeake Bay, Maryland.

MYSTIC CAT

Oscar the cat has correctly predicted the deaths of over 50 patients at the Steere House Nursing and Rehabilitation Center in Providence, Rhode Island, by curling up next to them some two hours before they die. For more than two years, he was present at every death in the home—except one when relatives asked him to leave the room. Nurses once placed Oscar on the bed of a patient they thought was close to death, but he immediately went to sit beside someone in another room. The cat's judgment proved better than that of the medics, because while the second patient died that evening, the first lived for two more days.

HOLMES MYSTERY

While in a trance in Winnipeg, Canada, in 1929, Scottish medium Mary Marshall produced nasal ectoplasm at the center of which was a face that her spirit guide—Walter—claimed was that of Sherlock Holmes creator Sir Arthur Conan Doyle, himself a confirmed believer in spiritualism. The necklace worn by Mary in the photograph is an "apport"—an object that materialized during the seance, but was not there before or after the event.

plain of jars Hundreds of ancient stone jars, some weighing up to 6 tons, can be found scattered across several square miles in northern Laos. Their purpose remains a mystery, but they may have been used to house the bodies of dead people until decomposition, after which the remains would have been removed for burial or cremation.

crystal tears Between March and November 1996, a 12-year-old Lebanese girl, Hasnah Mohamed Meselmani, produced glass crystal tears from her eyes. She wept tiny crystals at an average rate of seven a day, and although they were razor-sharp, she felt no pain. Physicians were mystified by her condition, which stopped as suddenly as it had started.

bacterial rain Over a three-week period in August 1994, gelatinous blobs rained down over Oakville, Washington State, leaving animals dead and people with flu-like symptoms. The blobs contained human white blood cells and two types of bacteria, one of which is found in our digestive system, but no one knows where the blobs came from.

GRAVE VISITS

When ten-year-old Florence Irene Ford was buried after dying of yellow fever in 1871, her distraught mother Ellen had steps built down to the head of the casket and a glass window installed so that she could comfort her child during the thunderstorms that had always terrified her during her short life. On many nights, Ellen would ride up to the cemetery in Natchez, Mississippi, and go underground to sit with her dead daughter and read or sing to her.

In the early 1990s, a woman took her 13-year-old daughter to visit the Ford grave at night. After descending the steps, the woman suddenly emerged screaming with a strange green glow all over her. As she rolled on the grass the glow diminished until a cemetery worker was able to scoop it into his hands. He later said it felt like compressed air or a tennis ball. He then released it into the air where it went up, sparkled, and disappeared.

Ripley's Believe It or Not! strange stories

human punchbag Xiao Lin, a fitness coach from Shenyang, China, rents himself out as a punchbag for stressed women who want to let off steam. The women pay $15 for a 30-minute session during which they can hit him as hard and as often as they like.

mother cat Peter Keonig, a Buddhist bank robber serving five years for armed robberies in Germany, had his request for his cat to be granted visiting rights to him in jail rejected by a court—despite his plea that the animal is the reincarnation of his mother.

bearly believable! A 2010 survey showed that more than one-third of British adults still take a childhood teddy bear to bed with them at night.

cool customer A man walked into a restaurant in Warren, Michigan, with a 5-in (12.5-cm) knife sticking in his chest and calmly ordered a coffee. The 52-year-old, who had walked a mile to the restaurant after having been stabbed, did not complain of any pain and simply told staff that he was waiting for an ambulance to come to care for him. Following treatment in a hospital, the man was expected to make a full recovery.

Upside-down House A totally upside-down house opened as a tourist attraction in the grounds of a zoo in Gettorf, Germany, in 2010. Standing on a pointed roof and supported by steel beams in the attic, the 23-ft (7-m) house boasts an upside-down kitchen, as well as a completely inverted bathroom, living room, and bedroom. Workers screwed 50 separate pieces into the "floor" (actually the ceiling), including beds, tables, and a microwave oven. Needle and thread were used to keep bed linen in place.

dancing cop Dressed in police blues, white gloves, and an officer's cap, Tony Lepore dances while directing the traffic at an intersection in Providence, Rhode Island. He began his dance routine in the 1980s through boredom and although he retired from the police department in 1988, he returns each year for two weeks to entertain passersby.

own juror William Woods was about to stand trial in Ottawa, Ontario, Canada, in 1999 on charges of dangerous driving, but the trial had to be postponed because Woods was summoned for jury duty—for his own case.

snake smuggler After customs officers in Kristiansand, Norway, discovered a tarantula in the bag of a ferry passenger who had traveled from Denmark, they decided to conduct a full body search. On investigation, they also found 14 royal pythons and ten albino leopard geckos taped to the man's torso and legs.

cash flow A 47-year-old Ukrainian man got his arm stuck in a public toilet in Chernigov for three hours after trying to retrieve $24 that he had dropped. With the man trapped up to his elbow, rescuers had to use hydraulic shears to cut him free. He emerged unharmed but $24 poorer, while the toilet itself was completely destroyed.

great survivor Frano Selak, a music teacher from Petrinja, Croatia, cheated death seven times, surviving three car accidents, two bus crashes, a train crash, and even a plane crash—accidents that otherwise left 40 people dead. His run of good luck continued when he won $1,000,000 in a lottery. To give thanks for being the luckiest man alive, he gave away his winnings to family and friends.

subway hideaway A 13-year-old boy who thought he was in trouble at school spent 11 days hiding on the New York City subway in 2009. Francisco Hernandez Jr. hid on the D train he normally rides during his short commute from his Brooklyn home to school. He slept on trains and survived on junk food he bought from newsstands along the route.

HEAD FOR HEIGHTS
A six-year-old boy slipped through window bars of an eighth-floor apartment in Hubei Province, China, but ended up dangling by his ears 60 ft (18 m) above the ground after they got trapped in the bars because the rest of his head was too wide to pass through.

surrounded city Although the city of Carter Lake is in Iowa, it is surrounded on three sides by the city of Omaha, Nebraska, and on the fourth by the Missouri River. It was formed by a flood that straightened the course of the Missouri and is the only city in Iowa that lies west of the river. It even gets its utility services from Nebraska.

pillow talk In a special ceremony in March 2010, Korean Lee Jin-gyu married a large pillow adorned with a picture of female Japanese animated character, Fate Testarossa. He put the pillow in a wedding dress for the service, which was conducted before a priest. He takes the pillow everywhere—and when he and his pillow bride go to a restaurant, the pillow gets its own seat and its own meal.

cesspit hell A Chinese man was rescued in 2010 after spending two days stuck up to his neck in a toilet cesspit. The man had slipped while using an outhouse toilet in Wuyuan, Inner Mongolia, and had fallen into the pit below. Unsurprisingly, as soon as he was freed, he ran to a nearby pond to have a wash!

wonder well Chand Baori, a 100-ft-deep (30-m) stepped well in the village of Abhaneri, Rajasthan, India, was built more than a thousand years ago with 13 stories and 3,500 steps.

bike burial When Harry "The Horse" Flamburis, a Hells' Angels motorcycle club leader from Daly City, California, died, he was buried with his motorbike.

LIVELY LANDINGS......

Is it a Bird?

Giant 300-ton Boeing 747s coming in to land at Princess Juliana Airport on the Caribbean island of Saint Martin fly just 60 ft (18.4 m) above the heads of vacationers on Maho Beach. They fly so low that they blow sand into the faces of plane spotters gathered below. The beach is right next to the runway, which, at 7,054 ft (2,170 m), is the shortest in the world to regularly accommodate 747s.

Over the autobahn
Leipzig Hall Airport, Germany

Low tide
Barra Airport, Scotland

Crossing the highway
Gibraltar Airport

Smoothed ice and snow
Ice runway in Antarctica

ACKNOWLEDGMENTS

COVER (r) Courtesy of Caz Housey; 4 Courtesy of Caz Housey; 8 (t) DeWitt Webb/www.cfz.org.uk, (b) Fortean Picture Library; 9 (t) Fortean Picture Library, (b) Tony O'Rahilly/Rex Features; 10 (t) © Illustrated London News Ltd/Mary Evans; 11 (b) Quirky China News/Rex Features; 12 (b) © 2009 Heiner Muller-Elsner/Focus/Eyevine; 12–13 (t) Henrik Lauridsen, Kasper Hansen, Michael Pedersen and Tobias Wang; 13 (t) Henrik Lauridsen, Kasper Hansen, Michael Pedersen and Tobias Wang, (b) Quirky China News/Rex Features; 15 (t) www.suzanneproulx.com; 16 (t) Shizuo Kambayashi/AP/Press Association Images, (c/l, b/l, b/r) JPL/NASA; 17 Kamioka Observatory, ICRR (Institute for Cosmic Ray Research), The University of Tokyo; 18 (t) Leon Shadeberg/Rex Features, (b) Courtesy of Caz Housey; 19 Fortean Picture Library; 20 Andy Willsheer/Rex Features; 21 (t) © Europics, (b) Charles Eisenmann Collection/University of Syracuse; 22 Claire Carter; 23 (t) © Bettmann/Corbis; 24 (t) Ibon Mainar/Rex Features, (b) www.sell-my-photo.co.uk; 25 SSPL via Getty Images; 26 Pictures courtesy of Vladimir Rogozov; 27 Kai-Hung Fung/Barcroft Media Ltd; 28 Reuters/Sean Yong; 29 Quirky China News/Rex Features; 30 (t) Fortean Picture Library, (b) Stew Milne/AP/Press Association Images; 31 (t/l, t/r) Fortean Picture Library, (b) Pictures courtesy of Donald Estes/Natchez Cemetery; 32 Quirky China News/Rex Features; 33 (t) Fabi Fliervoet/Solent News/Rex Features, (c/l) Flughafen Leipzig/Halle GmbH/DPA/Press Association Images, (b/l) Cover/Getty Images, (c/r) James D. Morgan/Rex Features, (b/r) Getty Images; BACK COVER DeWitt Webb/www.cfz.org.uk

Key: t = top, b = bottom, c = center, l = left, r = right, sp = single page, dp = double page

All other photos are from Ripley Entertainment Inc.
Every attempt has been made to acknowledge correctly and contact copyright holders and we apologize in advance for any unintentional errors or omissions, which will be corrected in future editions.